Dead Language

A Journey Through the Underworld

poems by

Jeanne Emmons

Finishing Line Press
Georgetown, Kentucky

Dead Language

A Journey Through the Underworld

Copyright © 2025 by Jeanne Emmons
ISBN 979-8-88838-990-4 First Edition
All rights reserved under International and Pan-American Copyright Conventions. No part of this book may be reproduced in any manner whatsoever without written permission from the publisher, except in the case of brief quotations embodied in critical articles and reviews.

Publisher: Leah Huete de Maines
Editor: Christen Kincaid
Cover Art: Jeanne Emmons
Author Photo: Lynn Nordsiden
Cover Design: Elizabeth Maines McCleavy

Order online: www.finishinglinepress.com
also available on amazon.com

Author inquiries and mail orders:
Finishing Line Press
PO Box 1626
Georgetown, Kentucky 40324
USA

Contents

I. Undertaking

Your Latin 1
Underclothes: Shopping for a Dress to Bury You In 2
Asunder 3
Turnings 4
Blind 6
Undertaking 7
Undercover 8
Packing the Underwear 9
Descent 11
Wunderworld 12
Underdogs I: Cerberus 13
Underpass: Crossing 14

II. The Gates of Ivory and Horn

The Gate of Ivory 19
Garden of Earthly Delights 20
Wunderland 21
Escher Underworld 22
The Gate of Horn 23
To My Mother as a Child, Waking 24
My Mother, at Six, Speaks to Me 25
Understudy 26
Underlining 27
Underdeveloped 28
Underlit 29
Undermine: Digging for the Dead 30
Underpinning: Your Constellation 31

III. Lethe

Under the Weather 35
Undercurrent: Lethe 36
Underdogs II: Bloodhounds 37

Underdogs III: Hounds of Heaven 39

Understanding 40

Undersea 41

Undertow: The Sea of Lethe 43

Blunder 45

Underdone 46

Underwood 47

IV. Dark Wood

Dark Wood 50

Undercarriage 51

Plunder 52

Undernourished 53

Understory 54

The Good Queen 55

Under the Illusion 57

Underwritten 58

The Origami of Grief 59

Under the Solar Eclipse 60

Hide and Seek 61

Tabu 63

Totem 64

Underlying 65

Sub-lingual: Dead Language 66

to Mother
in memoriam

I

Undertaking

> *Mortal, whate'er, who this forbidden path*
> *In arms presum'st to tread, I charge thee, stand,*
> *And tell thy name, and bus'ness in the land.*
> *Know this, the realm of night—the Stygian shore:*
> *My boat conveys no living bodies o'er....*

—Virgil, *Aeneid*, Book VI, Tr. John Dryden

Your Latin

Your love was our native language,
a word daily conjugated up and down
the stairs of our house, *amo, amas, amat,*
the sound of it embedded as deep in the walls
as the smell of Daddy's pipe smoke.
Everything afterwards was only derivation.
Even as you declined us, you embraced us.

In and out of school, *Magistra,* you
inscribed us with the fine red nib
of your intelligence, composed us with
the light tap of your chalk on the board,
so that the division of Gaul was a dogma
as certain as the three parts of God.
And the sweep of history always shushed
in our ears. Even the sound of the name
Caesar was like the stroke of your broom
on the linoleum of the kitchen floor.

Oh, *Mater,* how you did mother us.
We all knew without looking it up
where *gentle* came from—*gens: family.*
Those ancient etymologies planted so deep
in the lexicon of childhood, they carried
the entire genetic code of connection.
Now they unfold so fast that every day
seems a schoolday, and you rushing us
out the door. *Tempus fugit.*
Nunc eamus! Let's go!

Underclothes: Shopping for a Dress to Bury You in

The day after you died, the grief in my throat
unswallowed, I shopped for your last dress. You
had been so long in that dim room in muumuus

and sweatpants, your legs big as tree stumps
in compression hose that cut deep grooves,
your feet swollen out of your enormous shoes.

I wanted it to be floaty, feminine, with ruffles
or a bow, weightless, shimmering. Nothing
stiff like a suit. Something you could move in,

if you were going to move. Something you
would have worn with cologne and rhinestones,
blotting your lipstick, leaving that red kiss

on the tissue and me in my pajamas, adoring.
In the bridal shops, the clerks kept asking
when the wedding was going to be. Daddy loved

navy on you, and so I bought the midnight blue
in case he would be standing on the shore, in case
he would be free to hold you all decked out

in those fabric flowers and iridescent beads
to catch the light, if there were going to be light,
with chiffon sleeves to cover your bruised arms.

I refused the earrings with their clamps,
the hated bra, the shoes. And off you went,
Mother, in your closed boat, to float barefoot

and bare-legged beyond me, my dress-up
games, leaving me with all my grief undressed,
clutching this tissue with no visible kiss.

Asunder

Like flint to kindling, on the day you met
        at his parents' home, in nowhere, Louisiana,
                a spark flew up between the college dropout
        book addict with a thirst for Poe and Melville
and you, the smart new teacher with the pixie face.
        He was arrogant, insecure, brilliant, opinionated,
                and you, older, with your easy laugh and Latin,
        seemed out of his league. But you were so caught up
that when your college boyfriend proposed,
        you turned him down flat. After Daddy,
                all the others bored you, left you cold.

He worked to be worthy of you, finished school,
        then joined the army, earned his doctorate,
                became my father (always more your lover).
        And you were never asunder. How his eyes
would linger on your face, even as you aged,
        even as you kept on teaching, kept on grading,
                kept on coming home to fix his supper.
        You picked at your food, fell asleep on the couch,
went to bed early while he stayed up reading,
        his fierce pencil slashing through his dementia.
                Even with your failing knees and back,
        you hauled him in and out of his wheelchair,
and he would murmur *You're so beautiful.*

Your bodies lie parallel, separate now,
        cold, embalmed in wooden caskets, walled
                in vaults of concrete. If you were to wake
        suddenly at the trumpet sound on the day
of resurrection that you both believed in,
        your arms could never wrap around each other.
                I want to think you are somewhere else entirely,
        rejoined, embracing, folding and unfolding—
that in some strange spontaneous combustion
        you have felt the spark ignite, explode to flame,
                two tongues of fire braiding up together
                        into one, bright, pulsing column of light.

Turnings

1.

I've packed up Mother's things,
made calls, run my errands. Now,
stopped for a train, I have all this time
to watch the steel boxes rumble by,
their rust reclaimed by graffiti, its bright,
fat letters. The grooved wheels screech
and squeal, always in the same direction,
locked onto rails worn to a shine by
turning. My thoughts idle, window
open to December fog, the scorched
odor of the coffee factory, the smell
of sulfur in the mossy air.

2.

For miles, the flame from the refinery
pinks the underbelly of the fog. All night
that rose sky burns in the window, while I
lie sleepless on my girlhood bed, its canopy
dismantled in the closet, the pink eyelet cover
wadded in the corner. I turn and sigh and turn
the lamp on and off and on, now and then,
to read or sleep or watch the pink. At last,
my eyes close, my book drops to the floor,
and I know I have lost my place.

3.

This house moans under the burden
of its past, the soft contents divulged
to the light, then laid in cardboard boxes—
scrapbooks, crocheted bedspreads, first editions,
all turning yellow. Come morning, I step
outside for the paper. A baby frog the size
and color of an old penny hops across
the concrete, just the kind we used
to catch at recess near the ditch behind

Spindletop Elementary, only a few days
past tadpole stage, its whole life ahead.

4.

Around the old neighborhood, porch roofs
sag with termites, rot and mold, everything
groaning for rehabilitation, like the convicts
up the road at the house of corrections,
where the razor wire curls above a chain
link fence, turning on itself in a coil
of shine, sharp, keeping the threat
barely in check. It will have to do. I turn
the pages of my paper and sip the dark
roast coffee of my mother's kitchen—
hot, sweet, spiked with cream,
complicated, thick on my tongue.

Blind

I stood in the kitchen, once, Mother,
and watched you wash your hair, how it fell
forward into the full sink. You rinsed
and wrung it out, twisting it in your fists,
and a braid of water trickled with the lilt
of someone speaking in another room.
Your eyes shut. Your hand groped
for a towel. And then the cloth
concealed your face.

Once you were sleeveless in your summer
blouse, and the wicker basket of wet laundry
sat on the jut of your hip. I spun around
in the shade between the clotheslines, dizzy.
The sheets sagged on either side until
the wind gusted, the fabric billowed.
You were hidden behind the white and I
was alone, with a cool damp grazing my skin.

Now, without you, these recollections,
like snags in a stream, catch at my days,
My canoe glides in silence toward the shade
of a leaning willow with its tresses trailing
in the water. Then, from the other side,
the wingbeat of a great blue heron
drums the air, flaps and pulls upward
from behind the veil.

What shall I do with you gone?
I might cut the willow wands and make them
into a basket for memories or laundry.
I might even weave some wickerwork
to capture the bend of your body over the sink,
or the arch of your back reaching to fasten
a clothespin. I might knit a net of words,
but nothing will keep you. You will go on
escaping me, lifting up and moving
downstream each time I near you.

Undertaking

At the temple of Demeter in Eleusis,
the ground gapes into a hollow
through which, they say, Hades
thundered up and snatched Persephone
at her flower-gathering, her basket flying,
all the paper white narcissi scattered
in the hot slipstream of his chariot.

I tell myself you don't have to be a virgin
the gods lust for. Anyone can undertake
that journey, from anywhere. It's a matter
of mindset. Unfettered regret. Failure to forget.
But then I think otherwise. The dead turn
a cold shoulder to the living. And I hear,
if you make it that far down, no one escapes.

Except for Theseus, Orpheus, Hercules,
Odysseus, Dante, Psyche, Aeneas, Alcestis,
even Persephone, for the warmer months.
Oh, and Jesus and all the souls he harrowed
out of hell. Let there be no mistake. I want
to be in the illustrious company of those
who found their way back aboveground.

I fear Lethe, its current, the expunging
plunge. I'm afraid of being fastened
forever to the chair of forgetfulness.
I am going there solely to remember.
But I have no Circe to give directions,
no vat of blood to raise you, Mother,
or open up your tight-lipped, waxy mouth.

Undercover

Even the sheet is too heavy for sleep.
When I try to descend to you, it drags,
catches on the stones of the slope
I stumble down looking to drowse,
slumber, foreclose or find you.

I think the slow, drifting silent ones
would turn their hooded heads, resent me,
give me wide berth. Sleep resists me,
forces me to the side as the positive
poles of magnets repel each other.

I am restless for you. I do not belong
where you sleep, down there,
across that foul river. If I am to catch
a glimpse of you, I must go undercover,
pass as one of the dead.

Packing the Underwear

1. *Clothing*

I am rummaging through my closet,
the wire hangers, the jumble of shoes.
What does one wear, Mother, to go down there?
Shall I bring the seven pairs of underpants
you once gave me, one for each day of the week?
What will the weather be? Fire or ice,
a rain of shit, or the clear air of paradise?
I opt for layers I can peel off as things heat up,
a pair of jeans, a blue T-shirt, a hooded jacket.

2. *Headgear*

Something tells me a hat. And, though I already
feel the gravity of the upper world pressing,
it is not a hardhat or a helmet I want.
Just a black felt cloche with a feather
and maybe a net fascinator to hide my face
and the way my eyes will be scanning
the features of the dead for someone I recognize.
But all I find is this straw with a floppy brim
and a string and bead to keep it from flying off
in a high wind, a gardening hat, utterly pointless
for that deep shade, conspicuous, as if
I had imagined the sun might actually be
shining down there (though I *have* imagined it).

3. *Purse*

And what of the bag? Of those I have too many.
Canvas totes and old beaded clutches, a red leather
envelope with a cord handle and a big flap,
a black patent shoulder bag with the texture
of alligator pressed into its vinyl skin
and plenty of room for....what? A handkerchief

to wipe my tears? A change purse to hold
the coins for Charon? Enough folding money
to bribe Hades himself to let you
come back to me, if only for a season?

4. *Footwear*

And the shoes? For the rocky, steep, path down,
for stepping into the boat over the sucking marsh
of the Styx, to keep my feet from touching
the mud boils of the Acheron or the unruffled
erasures of Lethe endlessly smoothing her stones.
Not heels or flip-flops. This will be serious walking.

5. *Accessories*

The sneakers, then, and the garden hat
and the black bag, into which I throw
a handkerchief, a change purse,
pen, spiral notebook, granola bar,
three rawhide bones and dog biscuits,
one for each of the three heads of Cerberus,
the umbrella for the fecal downpour.
My hand hovers over the jewelry box,
and I choose your pendant of Lapis Lazuli,
to remind me of what I'm leaving behind:
the twilit sky, the sea of ultramarine.

Descent

It happens when I am on the verge
of sleep, that death in life we must
succumb to nightly. I'd imagined
a down staircase like the one
that opened up in the bedroom of
those twelve dancing princesses.
Every midnight they went underground
to waltz with their handsome partners
in the dark castle, then climbed back
up again at dawn, lining up their shoes
in tidy threadbare pairs beside their beds.
But there's only one of me,
and I have no ballet flats,
only sensible dream-sneakers
and the floppy hat of insomnia
always trying to fly off in the night wind.

Behind my eyelids the familiar purple
paisleys start to swim and plunge,
then elevator doors whump open,
and I step into absolute darkness,
no LL, G, B, no lighted button,
no raised star, no Braille, just
the sound of the doors meeting
and a sudden, stomach-dropping
descent into deeper darkness, cold.
And somewhere a winch whines
and something clanks and then
the squeak and high squeal of braking
and the clunk of the doors opening.
And my eyes need time to adjust
to the light of dreams by which
I hope to find you gliding lithe,
among the stalwart trunks and
shushing of the crape myrtle trees.

Wunderworld

I'm Dorothy opening the farmhouse door
expecting Kansas and finding Oz,
all Technicolor, lit by fluorescent
pendants that dangle from a low ceiling

painted to look like the sky, and the red-
orange of neon signs blink and point
this way and that. "Abandon All Hope,
Ye Who Enter Here," says one, but

the words rainbow over an enormous
eye that opens and closes in a slow
Wink, wink. On a billboard, an arrow
chases around the word "Sticks."

Another points to the "Elysian Feels"
and shows a giant hand rhythmically
squeezing a bulbous pink breast. You
would not be caught dead there, Mother,

and I feel a breath of unabandoned hope.
Maybe, after all, I won't have to cross
Lethe, won't have to forget you to find you
on the far shore of that subtracting stream.

Flowers bloom everywhere: red poppies,
moonflower, oleander, morning glories,
lily of the valley, belladonna, foxglove—
fragrant, beautiful, breathtaking, poisonous.

I must not swallow anything down here,
not even a seed, Persephone's fatal error.
On the other hand, nothing in this place
resembles Homer or Virgil or Dante.

I suppose they were all just making it up,
whereas this is reality, I think, as the world
around me alternately reddens and darkens
under that enormous neon eye. *Wink, wink.*

Underdogs I: Cerberus

Oh, but he stinks of infection, and his ruff
writhes and hisses. His serpent tail doubles
around and assesses me with eyes red
and hooded in a head the shape of a spade.
A forked tongue flicks back and forth
in an open mouth between two fangs.

As for his heads, there are three,
and each is in a different mood:
imperative, interrogative, subjunctive.
One barks incessantly, orders me
to turn tail and run. One whines,
begging for a pet, then cringes, his eyes
asking me who I am, why I am here.
One growls, a low, uncertain rattle, as if
I were hypothetical, contrary to fact.

I have come too far to turn back now.
I reach into my bag and feed each mouth
a dog biscuit between the rows of razor teeth,
then (wishing for steak) a rawhide bone.
I sidle past, and they gnaw resentfully,
their eyes fixed on hammer-hearted me.

Underpass: Crossing

I see now why they call it Sticks.
A beaver dam has clogged the stream
and made a sort of backwater estuary,
a bit of a wetland, where flotillas
of black swans backpaddle
and snake their necks around at me.

Points of chewed tree stumps and piles
of wood and twigs float and bob
in the murk. No sign of the actual beavers.
I could walk across, but I'm disinclined.
There could be piranhas, or quicksand.
The water might dissolve me.

I see him coming in his boat, rowing
for dear life. The keel grates on the shore.
"Are you the only one, Love?"
He peers closer. "Whoa! You can't fool
Charlie. I can't take you lot." His breath
reeks and wheezes through his rotting teeth.

His beard and jeans have seen too much
cleaning of fish, with blood and scales
stuck here and there. "I have my coin,"
I say, digging into my bag. He squints
at my penny. It might as well be a dog turd.
"Fare's gone up since Virgil," he says.

He blinks at me, then eyes my bag.
"Got any folding money in there, Love?"
I pull out a twenty, and he snatches it
and holds it up under a kerosene lantern
that hangs from a pole attached to his boat,
its light unreflected in the black water.

"All right, then, but don't tell nobody."
He reaches out his hand, and I step in
and stow my bag under the damp seat.
He pushes off with one of the oars,
swings us around, and starts rowing
into the steam of the stinking marsh.

I hear a ripple, a splash. I peer over
the gunwale and see the vague movement
of something pale, but it isn't her, and I
exhale. It quivers and disappears with
a flick of its flat tail. A paddlefish?
An albino beaver? Maybe.
Whatever it is, it's blind.

II

Gates of Ivory and Horn

> *Two gates the silent house of Sleep adorn;*
> *Of polish'd ivory this, that of transparent horn:*
> *True visions thro' transparent horn arise;*
> *Thro' polish'd ivory pass deluding lies.*
>
> —Virgil, *Aeneid*, Book VI, Tr. John Dryden

Gate of Ivory

I stray awhile. My trip veers
to nightmare. No itinerary,
no map, no brochure.
I come upon a gate
made of great tusks torn
from the face of some beast
massive and tortured.

Two bows of ivory touch
at the top, form a Gothic arch
rubbed to a shine by shoulders
of countless shades, carved
with phantasmagoria,
inlaid with gold.

When I pass through,
a glitz of anguish dazzles me,
all a delirium of neon sorrow,
unreal as the orangey makeup
they smeared on your face
to make you seem alive
and kissed by the sun.

Garden of Earthly Delights

after Hieronymus Bosch

I knew it would feel strange here when I came
down after you, Mother, but not so bizarre. True,
there is no one peeing into another's mouth.
No pale, naked people hatching from eggs, no
giant bird in a lifeguard chair like a tall potty seat,
eating people and pooping them out below while
another shits into the hole and another vomits
and has his forehead held by a woman grinning.

*

God no. Still, a man on a unicycle pedals by,
blowing very Bosch-like bubbles from his mouth,
one of which drifts towards me, its curved surface
squirming with pastels. Inside is a butterfly.
It floats closer still, and now it's *The Fly*
from 1958 and the insect has a woman's face
(not yours). She's alarmed, and mouths "Help Me,"
and I can barely hear her squeaky little voice.

*

And then the bubble touches my nose and pops
with a cold mist of tears, and a monarch flaps
away with orange and black wings and lands
on the bark of a tree with onyx leaves, and this
turns into a lute to which a man is tied, and
there is a shadowy woman strung up on a harp
and a bagpipe bladder on a plate atop a head.
And for the first time I think, *Let this be a dream.*

Wunderland

Now that I have finally followed you down here,
Mother, I can see that Charles Dodgson
must have been suffering some great grief

to let Alice fall into her deep rabbit hole all alone,
that corrugated vaginal wall slowing her descent.
Well, not quite alone, because he went after her,

invisible, tilting behind her back into that madcap
tea party, watching her sip oolong in the lap
of insanity with her unflappable manners.

What anguished tremor or monsoon of sadness
did he hope to quell in himself, setting
her among the mushrooms with her placid

sense browbeaten by caterpillars, vanished
cats with smiles extant, hedgehog balls
and swinging flamingoes? He was trying,

maybe, to work out some private conundrum
when he had her fend for herself with the cold
caterpillar, the mock turtle, the peppery duchess

while he came skulking after, taking it all down.
He wrote her reasonable beyond reason.
Maddeningly so. Calm to the point of lunacy.

But as I shadow you down, Mother, I have
no Alice to buffer me against the bizarre. I sniff
the air for a mere whiff of the Tabu you wore.

Instead, a picnic table materializes. A depression
glass plate piled with finger sandwiches—crustless:
ham salad, pimiento cheese. No pomegranate seeds.

A neon sign flashes *Eat Me*, and, though my famished
stomach yawns and spit floods my mouth, I turn
and run—lickety split—deeper into the absurd.

Escher Underworld

A ramp slants up and twists in an infinite
curve, a Möbius strip forever returning
to where it started. No beginning, no end,
no up, no down, self-involved, all surface.
And a woman (not you, Mother) treads it,
sometimes upright, sometimes upside down.
It seems not to matter to her. I call out, but
she does not turn her head. I do not believe
she sees me. Perhaps I am invisible here.

Nothing in this place is what I expected.
I thought dark, I thought dim and vapory.
I thought the smell of your perfume,
your arms, the murmur of your voice
taking me back to the feel of my body
in your lap, the floral pattern of the carpet,
the floor lamp that swayed on its base,
the soft skin-scented pages of a book of tales
all with a beginning, middle, and end,

where up was up and down was down,
where good was recognizable as you,
upright and true. And evil was downright
bad, and gravity pulled in only one direction.
It kept your feet to the ground, but did not
seem to bear down on your head, the way
it presses here, and there was always some
centrifugal force of faith, that counterweight
that meant a person could fall and rise again.

Gate of Horn

A gate of stone appears on the plain,
with two keepers I must pass between.
Each wears a leather belt and to it is tied
a humble ramshorn from the mountainside,
shed and retrieved on the steep scree of grief,
polished and carved with figures in relief.
When I pass, I hear the intake of breath,
and visions of true things in life and death
come one by one to mind, clear and detailed.
On the other side, a sudden wind exhaled
through sorrow's embouchure makes a moan,
steady and low, of two horns blown and blown.

To My Mother as a Child, Waking

That time you woke and found your mother
bending over you, her face inches away,
studying you with her eyes and mind unhinged,
you felt your heart jump with terror and love,
loneliness and need. How could you have known
that at that very moment, I had already flown
from the future back in time, riding on the wing
of your memories, the ones you would pass on to me,
to crawl under the covers of your twelve-year's bed,
and lay my head next to yours on the pillow of your fears.

My Mother, at Six, Speaks to Me

I am six years old, already too big, Daughter,
to fit under the mahogany buffet
of your imagination. My paper dolls
populate the space beneath. I kneel
in front to set them up inside the rooms
the eight legs make. I can feel you hovering.
I chew my lip and slowly turn a page.

You see my scissors pivot around the edge
of a baby carriage torn from the Sears catalogue.
I lean it against one of the wooden legs.
You watch me cut out a woman in a fur coat.
She's the mother. I try to stand her up,
but she wants to bend. I feel you always
trying to make something out of me,
because this memory I will pass on to you

will be too thin. You'll want to flesh it out.
It's not that you want me real. I'm real enough,
but that won't be enough for you. Here.
Take this page, these scissors. Don't keep on
pondering what to do with me. It makes me
feel flat, pressed inside something not me,
heavy, thick with desire, full of ideas.

Understudy

I am in a dark house, and I open a door
into this room, lamplit, full of thick books,
where I once practiced his part, her part,
thirsty, tipping the volumes back until
all the fluent syllables swam off the pages
into my head, possessed and overflowed me.

In this place the words are forbidden,
written in a lost and unfamiliar tongue,
all the titles unreadable, the gold leaf
worn down to the leather by too many hands,
even the vellum thinning. Underneath
their jackets, the hardbacks fray.
The pages of the paperbacks yellow
and crumble between their creased covers.

Back then, in the time of living,
the rolltop desk stood always open,
its pigeonholes full of pencils,
pipe cleaners, bottles of permanent ink.
Now someone has slid the lid shut,
each slat moving rough in its grooves,
pivoting and settling tight against
the next to close off whatever might
remain in there of him, of her.
The skeleton key is turned in the lock.

And I am left to declaim, dance, sing,
the main actor at last, playing the role
I always thought I wanted when I strained
to ease out from under their benign rule.
Now I'm bent under the burden of being
the principal in this production, my name
at the top of the marquee, improvising,
with no script but these sad scribbled notes.

Underlining

> *these are pearls that were his eyes*
> —Shakespeare, *The Tempest*

Down here in my grief, Father, I come upon
your books, your marginalia floating there
like a thing long submerged rising
to the surface, a bloated body
that belies the man.

    It was the worst of you. Your pencil
    slashed sarcasm, the question marks
    and exclamation points snaked and stabbed.
    It was the part of you that made me
    cringe, then made me stand up to you.

When the tide is at its lowest ebb,
what is left? The coral reef that forms
upon the armature of your true wit,
the bones of your righteousness,
the kind caverns.

    A hurt child might nestle in your armpit,
    or a baby squirrel in your hand,
    stray dogs you rescued wailing
    at the door, broken tomcats
    brought inside and tended.

I feel your emphasis, Father, in all of it,
the underlining that trenches the page,
and the flawed detritus, which loosens
from the text of you, bobs and stinks
and eddies away.

Underdeveloped

You said I was developing, Mother,
so you took me to buy my first bra,
confessing you had always felt flat-
chested, underdeveloped.
The department they called "Foundations"
sat in the middle of the store,
so everyone could see
a young girl fingering the lace.

How I longed to slip behind the slips,
disappear beneath the girdles and hose.
In the dressing room, you sat on the bench
while the clerk measured, kindly, delicate,
with her tape around my bare chest.
I cringed, too mortified even
to meet your eyes.

Now you are mortified, measured and fitted,
entrenched in the foundations.
Today I strain to find you where you live,
to fix your features. The old Polaroids
developed on their own, humming
out of that squat box, the image
a ghost at first until you waved your hand
and the picture deepened in color, clarity,
flushed to life.

But your face pales, recedes,
undevelops. You fade, blanch and blur.
With a buzz and whir, you withdraw again
into the narrow slot of the *camera obscura*.

Underlit

Nothing is punctual, Mother, least of all
memory. Your face under the lamp
of the past glimmers out of the dimness,
worms its way into the light, comes on
slow, then blurs back to gloom.

Even at lightspeed, lightning drags.
The burn of stars lags even longer.
For all we know, they might be dead
as bones, collapsed to the tight fists
of black holes, letting go of nothing.

So much of you is lost to me now,
all your benighted, belated lights.
Down here, in the dark of your death,
gravity rules, sucks everything in.
No light escapes. No stars at all.

Undermine: Digging for the Dead

How can such a dark, narrow place be so full
of diamonds, and where does the light come from
that winks and blinks on the rough walls?
Is it only this acetylene flame at my forehead,
the carbide lamp of the frontal lobe?

If I dig too far, too deep, won't the roof
collapse and crush me in a gravel-pile of gems?
Is there no limit to how far down I can go?
Won't this pickaxe eventually grow dull, break?
Won't my fingers bleed, stripped of their skin?

And suppose I should emerge with a drawstring
sack full of you. I could spend the rest of my life
sorting those nuggets, chipping at your inclusions,
flaws, facets, and still never have a jewel of absolute
clarity nor cast enough light for you to prism apart.

Underpinning: Your Constellation

From the first, our sapient species
ached for connection, picked out

the brightest stars, pinned them,
made imaginary lines to link the points

and bind the extant light of archaic suns
with filaments from our collective dreams.

We craved order, arranged a net of knots,
to spell something that might mean:

patterns visible only from the vantage
of home, third planet from our still

burning sun in a universe of trillions.
We couldn't help, it seems, but construct

this fancy lacework, tatted out of fictions
that we could fathom, manage to believe in

and use like blind guides in the dark.
So here, Mother, I astrologize you.

I link the scattered lights you left me:
the clothespins on the line, the swell

of the sheets, the red marks of your pen
on a student's page, the jumbled scents

of scarves and hose in your dresser drawer,
the crusts you trimmed from sandwiches,

the way you cut an apple crosswise
so the seeds in the center formed a star.

Let me pin down the sporadic firefly throbs
of memory to make some kind of sense.

Let me fabricate a web from all these bits
of raveling twisted yarns, to catch your drift.

III

Lethe

In Lethe's lake they long oblivion taste,
Of future life secure, forgetful of the past.

—Virgil, *Aeneid*, Book VI, Tr. John Dryden

Under the Weather

I'm peering across a lake ruffled with wind,
looking for you, and I think I see you dabbling
your toes in the water, dreaming of something
with that familiar faraway smile on your face.
It begins to rain, and you do not move. Your hair
goes flat and then streams with water, and the lake
is rough now, its waves washing over your knees.
And then the rain is a veil behind which you smile,
just as before, just before you dissolve.

Undercurrent: Crossing Lethe

I am threading a creek bed full of boulders, hopping
from one flat rock to the other without wetting
my feet in the narrow trickle in the middle, water
the color of breastmilk, translucent, almost blue.

I reach the other side and something rumbles.
Lightning spears down. Electrifies me. Leaves me
charged. Raindrops like pellets of jelly or falling frogs
plop around me and drench my hair and clothes.

I dig in my bag for the umbrella I would never
have brought except for the low murmur of your voice
in my memory, Mother. I open it, and rain globules thud
on the nylon membrane. A curtain of water encircles me.

The milky trickle grows to a rivulet, a stream shifting
the stones. I back up the slope, watch it seethe and swell.
I climb onto a boulder and fold up my knees. Milk rises
and foams, spits droplets, washes my island of stone.

In the rain-shadow of the black umbrella, I huddle and wait
for oblivion to engulf me, but the storm forgets itself.
The river settles down and slides by, swift and smooth
as a swath of satin. I cannot think how I will cross back over.

Underdogs II: Bloodhounds

I'm in a meadow underground.
The grass has soaked my jeans with dew.
The sun burns. Not a shade of sound
has brought to light a trace of you.

I don't belong. I'm of the living.
Who am I to seek the dead?
Who am I to want forgiving,
quick of heart and full of dread?

A sudden shudder shakes the weeds.
Flies scatter, grasshoppers flit.
In the distance something speeds,
rushing toward me, lickety split.

A slash in the prairie to my left,
a slice to my right. I turn. Behind,
the grasses part, then close, as if
something's escaped the meadow's mind.

From everywhere, beings malign
converge on me. A sudden shade
darkens the meadow. Bees whine,
my terror swells, my griefs invade.

Dolphin-like, a black shadow
breaches the sea of chicory blue,
then dives, then leaps again. The yellow
black-eyed Susans split in two.

A shape surges out of the grass
and then is once again concealed,
then lunges from a pinkish mass
of flowers, then plunges, unrevealed.

And from behind I hear a sound,
a panting, then a piercing bark.
A hound of hell! I turn around
to face its form, furred with dark.

I recognize him. He has found me,
springs! I know that massive head.
Then all the other dogs surround me
I have loved and walked and fed.

Shadow, Lance, Mabel, Pearl.
They lick my hands, their tails reel,
and the odors of damp dog unfurl
and romp in the Elysian Fields.

Underdogs III: Hounds of Heaven

Somehow, they remember me,
their tails wagging even as
their tongues lap up great gulps
of the waters of Lethe.
Perhaps all they forget is the fleas,
or the leash, the kennel, the shots,
the neutering. Maybe they do not
recall the cringing, the commands:
Come, sit, stay, roll over, fetch, beg.

I wonder now if you, Mother, absent-
minded, smoothed like a stone
in that river, might even so
summon up the memory of me,
maybe, unmarbled from my mistakes,
and forget only my faults, all
my lapses slipping your mind the way
these dogs in their oblivion overlook
my old orders and cold oversights.

Understanding

> *"the unplumbed, salt, estranging sea"*
> —Matthew Arnold

I have been walking for hours now,
contemplating Lethe's luxuries, the depths
of its warm waters, its smooth, opaque surface.
I could wade in and lift my feet from the bottom
and float, ferried downstream to blessed forgetfulness.

I could kneel and drink and sink into the milky sleep
of infancy and never care if you did not come, erase
what I know of you and will never know, never have
to scan your face or uncrypt its code. Oh, to unlearn
the reproofs you withheld, the unearned love you lavished.

But I do not wet my feet. I will not lose you to find you.
The river widens to a mouth, gapes into a delta, cries
into a gulf. The waves rush and foam, call me home.
I take off my shoes, but do not wade. This I understand:
The river of milk was only the beginning of Lethe.

Now I know it feeds into an entire ocean of forgetting.
A vastness of erasure. Deletion so deep you can't begin
to fathom its oblivion. Shoreless. No horizon. No floor.

Undersea

On this stretch of subterranean sand,
I keep walking, looking for my mother.
The ocean's full of whitecaps, and the surf
rolls and curls toward shore, then flows backwards
with tumbling clumps of green sea-grasses
and shells cartwheeling. This sun dazzles
but can't be real, must be a lamp suspended
from a ceiling painted blue. I can feel
my pupils contract to tight pinheads of pain.

I blink and see dozens of young couples
lounging on army blankets, olive drab wool.
A man stands with his back to me, raises
a Kodak 35 mm, puts his eye up
to the viewfinder, and points it at his friend,
who wears baggy, soggy trunks, and grins.
A private whose privates now must shrink
from the cold and wet of his suit, but one day
will enlarge, engorge, engender me.

I recognize him from the wedding album
they kept in their bedroom closet, those pages
I dipped into over and over as a child.
He picks up a woman in a damp one-piece,
and she reclines in his arms, her small breasts
against his chest, legs outstretched, those thighs
from which I will one day slide into the light.
She laughs, shades her eyes with her hand.

I hear the crunch of the shutter, the irising
of the lens in slow-motion. Down here,
the aperture is always small, the depth
of field infinite. I can see past her squint
and the man grinning, all the way until now.
They do not see me. The sun is too bright
behind me, perhaps. For them I do not yet exist.

The image blurs and swims. They have nothing
to do with me, so blissful that, even if they
could hear me, I could not loosen my tongue
to tell them where they are, have always been.

Undertow: The Sea of Lethe

I'm going in now, ready for the forgetting.
Water washes over my foot, the sand sucks
it down. Wave after wave undercuts me
until I'm up to my ankles, and still
I have not forgotten. I have not forgotten
that hospital bed, your vague, searching look,
morphine-dulled, raking my face.

Come, Lethe. I wade in. Each wave is a gut-
punch, nearly knocks me over. The sun
lights up everything, unmerciful. I want
to shield my eyes from your swollen legs,
muffle your voice ("are you leaving me?"),
the hair slicked back from that high forehead,
the skin taut and blue where you used to
comb your bangs above soft, appraising eyes.

Come, Lethe! I lift my feet and am carried out,
an undertow so strong the shore recedes.
It drags me into submarine rooms where
you sang to me, read to me, held my hand
into church, taught me in front of a blackboard
of Latin conjugations, stood at the stove,
sat hunched over your plate, picking, not eating,
sunk in the depression that dogged you.
You called me once in college, full of need,
and I could not talk to you, so stoned on weed
I only wanted off the phone. *Come Lethe!*

All the hurts you never blamed me for
hurt me now, and the joys, too, hurting.
How you read in the Sunday bulletin
And Jesus came before a great crow
and threw back your head in the pew.
Your gasping laughter shook the pious frowns.
And all that hilarity in our house when you
corrected student translations. "What else
did your mother teach you?" rendered as
"Who taught other mother?" The whole

family howling. *Come, Lethe.* You taught.
You taught other, Mother. This other.

In these milky waters I am out of my depth,
but nothing is erased. The undertow lets go,
and I am washed back through surf and cast
onto the shore. I lie and watch a mollusk
the size of my thumbnail upend itself
in the wet sand. It waits for the wash
of water, then extends its foot, digs in, sends out
its siphon to usher the ocean into itself, to sift it
and spew it out again, while the waves pound
and grind. I envy it. All it experiences, all
it remembers is that brine, passing in and out
through the narrow tube of its knowing.

Blunder

Lethe flows backwards now in the swift theft
of the receding tide, which sucks and wrests
oblivion away, a backward flood of gloom,
exposing a rough grotto, deeply recessed.

It beckons me. It sickens me with dread.
The TV on the wall, the cranked-up bed.
I feel my way down into the terrible room
where I last saw you, where so little was said.

You wanted me to stay and yet I left.
You weren't in pain, you said, or in distress.
I had a flight. I planned to come back soon.
You raked my eyes, but you did not protest.

If I had stayed, I guess I'd not have missed
asking if you were afraid, the lonely raft
of your body floating toward the edge of doom.
Did you hear the thunder of falls even as I left?

When I came back, your eyes were all adrift.
You lay in the arms of Morpheus, dispossessed.
You peered out bewildered from the plumes
of his dark wings, their feathered warp and weft.

And then the blue-scrubbed nurse glided soft
on his rubbery shoes and with a sudden, deft
hand plunged yet more sleep beneath your tongue
to slow, then stop your shallow, rhythmic breath.

I stumble out of the grotto. A foul draft
brings the stench of cigarette fumes that waft
from a figure in his blues lounging under
an overhang, a condor, an angel of death.

Oh, Mother, the marble stillness of your breast.
You wanted me to stay, and yet I left.
I had reservations. Unrefundable blunder.
I left you alone. You left me wholly unblessed.

Underdone: My Late Mother

1.

I should be over you, but I am not, am not done
with you, am underdone. How long may one
wear black, cover the head? How long before

the pale shoots of spring worm through
the frozen earth and petals open to expose
those pollen-studded depths to foraging bees?

How long before I am the bloom, before I am
the bee, sucking sweetness from the always
present moment? Mother, you are never finished.

The past keeps nosing into the now.
Those nights you sat on the flowered couch
and read me *Thumbelina,* your voice dawdled

on the way down to the conchs of my ears before
spiraling in, old sound, late as the counted seconds
from a lightning strike to the rumble of thunder.

2.

Even when I thought I had you, held your hand,
the face I looked up to lingered a nanosecond,
the image slightly delayed on the particles or waves

riding to my rods and cones, which reeled you in,
infinitesimally aged and changed. You were always
my late mother, trailing me, always past, never

fast enough to grasp in the flash of the moment.
All is nostalgia, and I, homuncula, undergrown,
long for your hand to lift and drop me down

into the gold-dusted funnel of the honeyed now,
to drink until I'm done. But when I bend to sip,
the dew of the present is always already gone.

Underwood

1.
You used that old typewriter to transcribe
Daddy's dissertation. Later I swiped it
for college work. It had no power cord,
no web, no server, and no motherboard.
But it served me well to tell stories, or fake
the chance poem out of life's inevitable ache.

Its steel mass squatted on my desk,
and, jabbing with my fingers, I possessed
the keyboard, punctuated the work. The back
key took you back, did not delete. I lacked
erasable bond. So I'd ponder each shade
of thought. I went slow, each stroke weighed.

Looking back, I'm amazed at how driven
I was, as the dimming ink on the ribbon
faded to gray. How I loved the ding of the bell,
that told in the high soprano of its small knell
that the line was done, that it was time to slam
the carriage return to the right and start again.

2.
The carriage return has now suddenly brought
me to the margin stop of a blacker underwood,
with underbrush and dense trees. I thought
surely I'd find you down here, but I could not.
I tried to forget you then, but couldn't. Strange,
to have bathed in Lethe, day after day, unchanged.

Only the dead forget, Mother. As for me,
a twisted cord connects the umbilicus of grief
to memory's placenta. My helpless fingers
tremble. This is an Underwood of unease.
I am still looking for you. I still linger,
hoping somehow to find the margin release.

Let me step from Lethe's flood plain of loss
into the understory of myrtle and moss,
quaking aspen, dogwood, and wild plum,
grapevine, redbud, bittersweet. Let me come
at last into the underwood and through,
beneath a canopy of shadows, cypress and yew.

IV

Dark Wood

> *Midway upon the journey of our life*
> *I found myself within a forest dark,*
> *For the straightforward pathway had been lost.*
>
> *Ah me! how hard a thing it is to say*
> *What was this forest savage, rough, and stern,*
> *Which in the very thought renews the fear.*
>
> —Dante, *Inferno*, Canto I, Tr. Henry Wadsworth Longfellow

Dark Wood

> *'Rise to thy feet,'* my Master said to me;
> *'The way is long and rugged the ascent,*
> —Dante, *Inferno*, Canto XXXIV

Dante entered through a dark wood,
but left climbing feet-first down
the goat-legs of Satan, fists clinging
to the frozen fur, making a sudden pivot
at the genitals, to climb upwards
and exit through an opening where
he saw the stars again.

I came here by plunging into the absurd
of your death, inside the claustrophobia
of a bare-walled elevator, unattended.
Arriving, I found no Lucifer ice-locked
in a frozen lake, only the dark
grotto of memory and regret,
that glimpse of your
uncomprehending face.

Now I must leave through my own dark wood.
I hear it rustling, speaking in tongues,
root, blade, and tip, beyond all sense.
But it sounds real, deeply understood,
sublingual, beneath language,
all else merely derivative.

Undercarriage

> *Because I could not stop for death*
> *he kindly stopped for me*
> —Emily Dickinson

Because I slowed my feet, because I stopped
for death at the side of the road and stood
still, because death was no gentleman, but clopped
up in his carriage from behind, high and proud,
caught up with me and passed and would not slow,
because I saw you beside him, facing forward,
because I ran after you, and you did not know
me, because I swung up onto the running board,
because you vanished then and left me alone
with no reins in a night too dark to see,
while the chassis underneath swayed and groaned,
because, Mother, you kindly did not stop for me,
I find myself at this wood where the road ends
and must somehow go on, on foot again.

Plunder

I climb over another rotting log
        fallen across the path to you,
                Mother. Something wants to block
      my way, keep me from the small
pink house of my childhood, with all
        the trees Daddy planted: oak and yew
                cottonwood, sycamore, fig, catalpa.
      When I arrive, it's all gone wild and made
a thicket of impenetrable shade.
        Saplings have sprouted in the sagging gutters.
                The blinds are down,
the windows all are shuttered.

Deeper into the understory, I'm still
        stumbling toward your heart, toward
                the big two-story, with those tall
      pines he dug as seedlings from the woods
of Louisiana, and brought back in coffee cans
      to plant for you in the back yard.
                Twelve of them outlived him and then,
      they fell together in a single storm,
all parallel to the house, taproots torn,
      from the ground. You and the roof were spared.
But when I come to it, no one is there.

And now I search for the house he built
      at the beach for you, weathered, up on stilts—
               the roof of tar, the rusted nails, the sand,
      nothing square. I look for those oleanders
and palms he planted near that stretch of land
      where Jean LaFitte rolled his barrels of plunder.
                When I reach the place, all is contraband,
      stolen by the draft of hurricane, the theft
of storm surge, whip of riptide. Nothing's left:
      but a concrete slab
and the sound of surf and thunder.

Undernourished

I thought I would starve down here, Mother.
Over and over, I have found food, but I am afraid
to ingest anything here below. I am not wanting to stay.

In this shadowed valley, the trees drip with moss,
overhang my narrow path beside the unmentionable
ravine that beckons like a drug. I want blinders.

No table has been prepared for me that did not reek
of toxic sweetness or the must of mushrooms.
My cup has not run over, except with poison.

But now there is a whiff of corn bread baking.
I follow it to a cottage in a clearing, a candy house,
forbidden, seductive, but not the place I long for.

You are no witch, and your oven is not meant
ever again to house my body. Through the wavy
pane of the sugar-glass window, I see you in shorts

and shirt, young again, dredging chicken. The flour
is a glove on your already pale hands. I know
you feel me staring, but you do not look up

from the black skillet where you lay each soft,
mound of dead flesh to sizzle in a half-inch
of grease. I sense you wanting to look at me,

as Orpheus was dying to glance back at Eurydice.
But you resist, protecting me, as always.
So I am left staring at the side of your face.

A breeze picks up in the linden trees behind me
bringing the faint sweetness of their blossoms
as you pull the cast iron pan out of the oven,

the cornbread gold and brown, with steam rising.
The smell alone is more than enough, you know,
to fill the bowl of my memory up to the brim and over.

Understory

It was always you who read me the story.
You spun my straw into gold.
You were the fairy queen,
the good godmother.
You knitted me
the shirts of nettles to make me
human again, left me the one wing.
You had the wand, the crown, the dress.
You carved me out of wood, made me a real girl.

All this time, I've haunted your underworld,
wanting you to come to me, face me,
outlive me, look me in the eye,
know me, forgive me.
But now I know it is my turn
to write you backwards. I am neither
a mirror nor a lamp. I have to build you
like a house, to shelter me, build you
like a fire, to warm me, even as you die,

compose you as you decompose, compose
myself, bring our duet back
into harmony after the long
caesura, the whole
rest, the bird's eye
of the fermata watching,
the empty measures of your death,
your fugue of silence. Oh, Mother!
How I have wished you to ghost me.

Today, I dissemble and invent
and reassemble you, or someone
resembling you, gather
and weld together
the rusty spare parts of all
that I've missed of you, draw you
into my disheartened arms and kiss you.

The Good Queen
to my mother

On my childhood's trail of loose dirt,
my dress-up skirts always dragging,
you followed behind, just
far enough that I felt
wholly alone, a dusty
princess in the sight
of the sycamore trees.
their rattling leaves
and the pinkish light
of sunset and the gusty
wind muffled between the quilts
airing and the sheets in those huffs
of air, billowing out and then sagging
on the line, the pegs like so many birds,

so many words spaced out. You wove
me nursery rhymes and tales. You cut
my apple crosswise so that a star
appeared, its arms full of dark
inedible seeds and the sweet
promise of some far life
too rich for my mind
to swallow. The rind
spiraled from your knife.
At the sink, with your bare feet,
shorts, and sleeveless blouse, the clock
always moving its three hands, you were
the good queen the fairy tales kept shut
in the woods and never spoke of at the stove

Now, even in the ever after and rough weathers,
with cherubim guarding the clean laundry,
the apple core and the cool orchard,
I can design no shadow nor blight
in that old garden, no breach
of innocence or nature.
I'll not deface you
so I will trace you
in crayon on manila paper.
You smile. Your arms reach
out of your curly head. Here are bright,
impossible flowers, the sun in the corner
with its yellow rays. And here are sprawling
loops spelling *MOTHER* in naïve, unmistakable letters.

Under the Illusion

It is warm and dark in this wood of lost tears.
The leaf-rot smell rises and sifts down soft
to the roots of infant trees. The smooth heads
of acorns shed their coarse caps, those topknots
and rims of curls that dignify them among
the homely, brown things of the earth. They crack,
and white sprouts squirm out, stretch up, grow wings.

I am finding my way in this wood of no stars,
following the true north of you home. I was
under the illusion death would leave no footprint.
Then, stomped and flattened under that impression,
I sniffed dread lurking beneath the bed of my grief.
Now I smell the sweetness of earth's common
compost and feel her arms open to embrace me.

I swear I can hear the little horns of fern
unwinding out of the dark, the green buds
boiling up on the bare limbs. I know that
one day, in this wood of no fears, I will be home.
But not today. It is time to close my eyes,
stretch out my arms, and ride the updraft of April
back to the cool sheets of what is left of my life.

Underwritten

You expressed me from between your thighs,
in a thick ink to form that first primer
of my childhood. You stroked the initial I's
onto the text of my life, made them shimmer,
illuminated in the red and gold of love,
the calligraphy of your fine longhand.
It was a fair draft, but I would make it rough,
overwrite it, smudge it with my own brand.

Oh, Mother, I blotted your letters over and over,
but you were always my author. Your cursive
curled in the meadows of my first dream, gestures
I would have erased until I abraded the paper
but for your breath bending each of my characters
to roundness, so the two of us together in time
cultivated the poem toward sense, rhythm, and rhyme.

The Origami of Grief

I have folded myself forward
and back again to find you,
bent diagonal and straight,
till I am nearly torn apart.
I have raised up a mountain
of mourning, furrowed a valley
of sadness, pleated my cries,
in repeated corrugations,
reversed and pleated again,
fashioned whole pockets
of lamentation, then tucked
myself into them, turned
myself inside out, crimped
my pain into sharp points.
And still no boat, nor goldfish,
no paper crane, no likeness of you.
All I want now is to undo myself,
lay me flat again, like a sheet
on a bed of healing, smooth out
the creases of my grief and sleep.

Under the Solar Eclipse

I was not prepared for the moon of your death
to blot you out so fast. It was predictable,
and yet I think my eyes would have required
dark shades to track the shrinking arc

of your life, the bulge of growing black.
I preferred to look at the world unfiltered,
in your ambient light, firefly-studded,
the dreamy dusk of your dimming.

Your voice on the phone murmured thoughts
still lucid, and your laugh caressed my ear.
I should have known how far the dark had grown,
your cataracts, swelling, congestion, brittle bones.

With my naked eye I saw, beneath the trees,
among the shivering shadows of the leaves,
hundreds of shining crescents. I felt the air
go suddenly cold, and still I did not believe.

And then the dome of dark descended fast.
A lid closed over the open pot of the world,
with just that band of light around the rim
to remember you by. And there I have been,

suspended in totality for all this time,
staring at the bright corona of your life,
its jewels embedded around a disk of black.
Now at last you emerge on the other side,

a diamond solitaire, a surge of light.
Here I release you from the dark sphere
that I know now was never your death, Mother,
but just the cold, pock-marked rock of my grief.

Hide and Seek

> *I have tried in my way to be free*
> —Leonard Cohen

That time you punished me, when I was four,
I hated you so. All morning I had been free
in my own way, beneath a wheelbarrow,
waiting for the older ones to find me.
Loneliness hurt me like a bodice
with its strings poisoned and too tight.
Then, all the in-frees over, I tagged along
behind the others down the street.
Brave with our numbers, we left no trail
even of bread to follow home.
We lost our way, were gone all afternoon.

For that, you banished me to the dungeon
of the screened porch, my heart fat with fury,
nearly cut out of my chest.
In my way, I had been free all day,
lagging behind with that shiver of risk
up and down slanted sidewalks where
whole sections were nudged up
by the roots of the live oak trees.
My short legs scurried, following the dwarves.

Now, you were the witch in the candy house.
and so I told you, rocking back and forth.
I spat the words like bits of unripe apple,
Wicked queen! How well I knew that hag
from books at bedtime, on the couch beside you,
my milk, the lilt and murmur of your voice.

Now I think you've floated there beside me
all my life in that transparent bubble,
holding a star-tipped wand. All my life,
in my way, I have been free, have fought
through forests, thickets of briars, have come
upon the house of gingerbread over and over,

as if by accident, and found it sweet.
It was always you I came home to.
You were the oven of warm bread.
It was always you who kissed me awake.
You were the mirror, the one who looked
upon my faulty, blemished form and said,
Darling, you are the fairest of them all.

Tabu

I have bought a bottle of Tabu,
just to remember you by.
This earthy scent, this dark
you dabbed behind each ear
and on the pulse of your wrists
seems to rise up out of the ground.

I have only to breathe, and you
are alive in hose and heels,
rhinestones and red lipstick.
Your permanent wave swirls
to conceal your face, and you
breeze out in a blur of Tabu.

Rose, jasmine, orange blossom,
amber, oakmoss, musk.
Even as a child in pajamas
I knew the secret smell.
Now you are again forbidden,
concealed in the cloak of your death.

You've closed the door of your room.
The tender voices are muffled.
And I am left with the bottle
I found in the drugstore, cheap,
boxed with dusting powder,
beside other passé perfumes
worn only by the very old,
or the forlorn daughters of the dead.

Totem

From Mother it came down to me, the small
hinged box of baby teeth she kept
from her three children, unsorted, all
unlabeled and collected while we slept.

Now, from my children's mouths, I have added
incisors, canines, molars I discovered
beneath the pillows where their heavy heads
were tangled up with dreams of wings and silver.

I snap the lid and wonder: Will our kin
in the far future dig out the pulp, unsettle
the DNA, and reconstitute their forbears,
all out of sorts and chattering in this tin?
Or will they seal them in some magic rattle,
a dried gourd—shaking—unhinged—disordered.

Underlying

I have not yet visited that plot of yours, Mother,
have averted my gaze from your body underlying
the earth, cramped into your moisture-resistant
box, with folded hands, sealed eyes and lips.

I try not to tell myself those truths, lying under
some delusion instead, always hoping for
an embrace, anticipating a kiss, a conversation,
a clasp of warm hands in a dappled light.

Odysseus descended, tried three times to hug
his mother's shade but could not. And Aeneas,
keen to enfold his father's underlying
flesh, felt his hands go through empty air.

How often will I have to open my arms to find you
absent? You seem a blanket of warmth I lie under,
a pillow of comfort, your voice a murmur, a balm.
But my arms pass through these sweet mirages

to wrap around my own solid inescapable self.
Where I imagine you are somehow underlying,
as your mother was in you, and she in hers, down
and down to our first mother. As I will underlie

my daughter and she hers, within each other nested,
womb within womb, heart within heart, to the last
daughter, whom all others underlie, who will not lie
curbed underground, but free, beneath the open sky.

Sub-Lingual: Dead Language

If someone said Latin was dead, it irked you
to no end, *Magistra*, so alive it was in you with
the blackboard behind you and the white chalk
declensions ranked in orderly columns and the clock
hand in your classroom sweeping above a sign
that read *Tempus fugit*. You raised your arms,
and taught us a Latin cheer for the football team.
At Christmas, your hands conducted *Silens Nox*
and *Adeste Fidelis*. Back home, at bedtime,
we whispered Ego *te amo* into each other's ears.

You are always under my tongue, *Mater,*
as alive as you insisted Latin was, against all
common sense, your roots still thriving deep
within the very lexicon of my life, thrumming
with your derivatives, your mammary grammar
my present perfect, imperative, subjunctive.

Since your passing, I have wished to believe
that the nouns of all five declensions,
with their modifying adjectives, participles,
and subordinate clauses, were marching
with quiet dignity toward that inevitable verb
biding its time at the end of the sentence,
reticent as some mystery, cryptic, withheld
until the veil would be lifted to reveal
the soar and flutter of action (*fugit*—she flies)
or some bright state of being *(est*—she is).

Acknowledgments

I gratefully acknowledge the following publications in which these poems, or versions of them, have appeared:

"Descent," *Oakwood*
"My Mother, at Six, Speaks to Me," *Alaska Quarterly Review*
"The Origami of Grief," *River Styx*
"Sublingual: Dead Language," *River Styx*
"Tabu," *Persimmon Tree*
"Totem," *Alaska Quarterly Review*
"Turnings," *The Sow's Ear Poetry Review*
"Under the Solar Eclipse," *Louisiana Literature*
"Underclothes: Shopping for a Dress to Bury You In," *Calyx*
"Underdeveloped," *Xavier Review*
"Undernourished," *Louisiana Literature*
"Understory," *Louisiana Literature*
"Undertaking," *Oakwood*
"Underwood," *Oakwood*

For their ongoing support and constructive feedback and for lovingly shepherding these poems from rough draft to completion, I am deeply indebted to the members of my writing group: Nancy Braun, Steve Coyne, Tricia Currans-Sheehan, Deb Freese, and Barbara Gross. I am also grateful to the following members of the Women Poets Collective for their careful reading of individual poems and thoughtful commentary on the arrangement of the manuscript: Jodi Andrews, Lysbeth Benkert, Darla Biel, Barbara Duffey, Heidi Czerwiec, Christine Stewart-Nuñez, Melinda Obach, Pen Pearson, Marcella Remund, Erika Saunders, and Norma Wilson. Thanks to Michael Moos, Marcella Remund, and Christine Stewart-Nuñez for graciously agreeing to read this book and comment for the back cover. Most of all I want to thank my husband, Adam Frisch, and my children, Austin and Eleanor, for their enduring patience, love, and encouragement.

Jeanne Emmons has published four previous collections of poetry: *The Red Canoe* (Finishing Line Press); *The Glove of the World*, winner of the Backwaters Press Reader's Choice Award; *Baseball Nights and DDT* (Pecan Grove Press); and *Rootbound*, winner of the New Rivers Press Minnesota Voices Competition. She received her PhD in English from The University of Texas. Her work has appeared in *Alaska Quarterly Review, American Scholar, Carolina Quarterly, Louisiana Literature, Poet Lore; Prairie Schooner, River Styx, South Carolina Review, South Dakota Review, Xavier Review*, and many other journals. She is the former poetry editor of *The Briar Cliff Review*. She lives on a lake in South Dakota with her husband and cat.

www.ingramcontent.com/pod-product-compliance
Lightning Source LLC
Chambersburg PA
CBHW030057170426
43197CB00010B/1558